PAUL W. POWELL

LAUGH AND LIVE LONGER

Good Humor to Brighten and Lighten Your Life

© Copyright 2008
Paul W. Powell
5603 Elderwood Drive
Tyler, Texas 75703

Printed in the United States

Dedication

J.D. Hudson
John and Ruth Wilkerson
Ray Wilkerson
J.L. "Sonny" and Gretchen Williams

Friends who have brought joy to my life!

Table of Contents

Introduction

A current television advertisement by a well-known insurance company pictures a baby laughing and laughing and laughing as his mother plays with him. Then a caption appears that says, "Laugh and add eight years to your life." A few weeks later a second ad by the same company pictured a religious symbol with a caption, "Have faith and extend your life three years."

I do not know about faith, but I am sure laughter not only adds to the quantity of our life, but to the quality also. The scriptures are explicit, "A merry heart doeth good like a medicine" (Proverbs 17:22). Someone put it this way, "Laughing is good exercise. It is like jogging on the inside." I like that.

There is no doubt humor helps us have a healthy outlook, a healthy body, and even healthy relationships. Daniel H. Pink wrote, "More than four decades of study by various researchers confirms some common-sense wisdom: humor, used skillfully, greases the management wheels. It reduces hostility, deflects criticism, relieves tensions, improves morale, and helps communicate difficult messages" (*A Whole New Mind*, by Daniel H. Pink, New York: Riverhead Books, 2005, 190).

Walt Garrison, who once played running back for the Dallas Cowboys, was asked if he ever saw coach Tom Landry smile. He replied, "No, but I've only been here six years." Landry, of course, did have a great sense of humor. But he was usually so absorbed in the management of the game he was coaching that he seldom showed any emotion, including a smile, while on the sidelines. If we aren't careful, we can get so caught up in the game of life that we forget to enjoy it and to enjoy ourselves as we go along.

So regardless of whether you are a coach, business man, teacher, or politician, we need to learn to laugh at ourselves and to laugh with others.

Ministers especially need to learn to laugh and to use humor in their sermons. As Herb Gardner reminds us, "Once you get people laughing, they're listening and you can tell them almost anything." That's the whole purpose of this book. It's a collection of good stories, almost none of which are original, that can be used on almost any occasion to help lighten and brighten your day and the day of those around you. So sit back, relax, and have a good laugh. Then pass them on to others. It'll be good for you and for everyone you encounter.

Paul W. Powell
George W. Truett Theological Seminary

Chapter 1

General

1. We've Never Been This Far Before

Two Jehovah's Witnesses rang the doorbell of a house. The man of the house answered the door and they identified themselves. He said, "Come on in fellows, and we'll visit." He took them into the living room and said, "Sit down there on the couch." They sat down and he said to them, "Now what did you want to tell me?" They said, "We don't know, we never got this far before."

2. We've Got to Stick Together

A group of people were riding on a train when a robber came into the car and began to take all of their possessions. He walked up and down the aisles stopping at each chair and demanding their valuables be placed in a large stack. Billy Graham happened to be on that car and when he came to Graham and his companions, the robber walked on by without demanding their money. As he turned to walk out of the train, Graham called out to him, ""Hey . . . wait a minute. Why didn't you take my possessions?" The thief responded, "I recognize you Mr. Graham, and we Baptists have got to stick together."

3. Helping God Out

A professor stood before his class one day and declared emphatically, "There is no God!" Then he said, "I'll prove it to you. If there is a God, I will give him five minutes to come down here and knock me off this platform."

The class was stunned to silence as the minutes ticked away. One minute, two minutes, three and nothing happened. The atheistic professor then taunted God by lifting his face up to Heaven and shaking his fist and saying, "God, I am waiting. If you are up there, come down and knock me off this platform."

Just then, a Marine fresh back from Iraq who had recently enrolled in the class, walked up to the platform and cold-cocked the professor, knocking him to the floor. When he got up and shook the cobwebs from his mind, he said, "Man, why did you do that?" The marine replied, "God was busy and he sent me to help him out!"

4. Dealing with Difficulties

A cowboy was sitting on a barstool one night, minding his own business, when a fellow came in and sat down beside him. Without any warning, the man reached over, whacked him across the back of his neck with the edge of his hand, knocked him from the stool and down on to the floor. He got up, looked up at the man, and said, "What was that?" The man replied, "Judo from Japan."

The cowboy continued with his drink, minding his own business, when the man next to him, for no reason at all reached over and hit him across the back with his forearm, knocking him from his stool and to the floor again. The cowboy got up, brushed himself off, and said, "What was that?" The man replied, "Karate from Korea."

Without a word, the cowboy went outside, came back in a minute and hit the guy that had hit him so hard that he knocked him off the stool and was unconscious for five minutes. When he finally came to, he looked at the cowboy and he said, "What was that?" The cowboy replied, "Tire tool from Wal-Mart."

5. Dealing With Children

I was in a grocery store recently and heard a man on the next aisle talking to his two-year-old son. The son had been crying, wanting this and that, and generally making a nuisance of himself. The man pushing him in a grocery cart kept saying to himself, "Just be calm, Albert. Don't lose your cool, Albert. Control yourself, Albert."

I stepped around the corner to commend the man for his patience and said, "Sir, I think it is remarkable the way you have controlled yourself so well in dealing with little Albert." He looked at me and said, "Sir, I am Albert."

6. It's Hot in Here

A man and his wife in Dallas were planning to celebrate their 20th wedding anniversary. They decided to go to Florida and stay in the same hotel, "The Honeymoon Hotel," that they had stayed in twenty years before. There was a mix-up in their travel plans and he had to go a day early. When he got there he immediately sent her an e-mail. The problem was, however, he sent it to an incorrect e-mail address. It was missent to a lady in Houston who had just returned home from the funeral service of her preacher/husband.

The e-mail read, "Arrived safely and was checked in immediately. They now have computers in this place and you are allowed to send e-mails to your family. I checked in without any problems and we are prepared for your coming tomorrow. I hope your trip is as uneventful as mine. Look forward to your arrival tomorrow. P.S., It's really hot down here."

7. Pressure – We're Under the Gun

An old mountain preacher was riding his horse down the road one day when he came upon a hillbilly with a jug of homemade Mountain Dew. The hillbilly said to the preacher, "I want you to take a drink with me." The preacher said, "That stuff has never touched my lips, and it never will." The old hillbilly reached over and pulled out his shotgun, pointed it at the preacher, and he said, "You take a drink of that or I'm going to shoot you."

So the preacher turned up the jug, took a big swig, and let out a scream, and said as he swallowed, "That's the worst tasting stuff I've ever had in my mouth."

The hillbilly said, "I know. Now, you take the gun, hold it on me while I take a drink."

8. I Hope You're Comfortable

In deep East Texas around Center, two farm ladies had lived on the farm all of their lives; they had never known very much until they struck oil and suddenly became rich. They went into town one day to a high class furniture store, at least the highest class in Center. As they were looking around, they saw a bowl of different colored leaves that smelled really good on top of a chest. And so one of them asked the clerk, "What is this?" And the clerk said, "That's potpourri." She said, "Well, what is potpourri used for?" The clerk said, "You put that in your drawers to make them smell good." And the country lady said, "Isn't that terribly uncomfortable?"

9. Don't Know Why You Came Today

A cowboy came to church one Sunday, fell under conviction, and when the invitation was given, he went forward to join the church. The pastor baptized him that night and the church rejoiced at receiving a new disciple. Their pastor heard the next Saturday night, however, that the cowboy had been out to a night club and been dancing that Saturday night. So, the pastor called him and said, "Bill, now that you've joined the church, you need to know that we don't go to places like that and do things like that. That's not the Baptist way."

Bill responded, "Pastor, I didn't know that. When I joined the church, nobody told me that I shouldn't do things like that. When I went down to the front I didn't read anything about that on that little card. Then they baptized me Sunday night, but nobody mentioned that to me. But, Pastor, it won't be any problem. The fact is, I don't like to dance and I wouldn't even had been there if I hadn't been drunk."

10. You've Got to Think Fast

A man walked into the produce section of his local supermarket and asked to buy half a head of lettuce. The boy working in that department told him that they only sold whole heads of lettuce. The man was insistent that the boy ask his manager about the matter. Walking into the back room, the boy said to the manager, "Some moron wants to buy half a head of lettuce." As he finished his sentence, he turned to find the man standing right behind him; so he added, "And this gentleman kindly offered to buy the other half." The manager approved the deal, and the man went on his way. Later the manager said to the boy, "I was impressed with the way you got yourself out of that situation earlier. We like people who think on their feet here. Where are you from, son?"

"Texas, sir," the boy replied.

"Well, why did you leave Texas?" the manager asked.

The boy said, "Sir, there's nothing but prostitutes and football players down there."

"Really?" said the manager. "My wife is from Texas."

"No kidding," replied the boy. "Who'd she play for?"

11. You Can Believe the Bible

A school teacher was speaking to her third grade class and they were talking about animals, and she remarked that it was completely impossible for a whale to swallow a person. She pointed out that while the whale was very large, the size of its throat was such that a person could not slip through it. One little boy said to her, "Teacher, that's not true. The Bible says that Jonah was swallowed by a whale. And if you don't believe it, I will ask him."

The teacher responded, "Suppose, when you get to heaven, Jonah is not there?"

The young boy responded, "In that case, you ask him."

12. I Need Help

A young man was being interviewed for a job as a policeman. As his superior asked him questions about the various experiences he might have, he said to him, "What would you do if you were called upon to arrest your own mother?"

Without hesitation, he said, "I'd call for backup."

13. Texas – A Local Call

A Texan in New York City wanted to make a call back to Texas and he asked the operator how much it would cost. She said, "$7.35 a minute." He said, "My goodness. That's terribly expensive. I don't usually argue about cost, but in Texas we can call Hell for less than that." She said, "Yes sir, but in Texas that would be a local call."

14. Tonsils – Not Where You Think They Are

Two little boys were talking one day and one said to the other, "I've got to have my tonsils taken out next week." His friend responded, "Well, so do I. I have to have mine taken out in two weeks. Maybe you can tell me how it feels when your operation is over."

The next week the parents took the first boy in to have his tonsils removed. Once the doctors had administered the anesthetic, the parents said, "Doctor, when he was a baby we failed to have him circumcised. We were wondering if while you are removing his tonsils, you could circumcise him at the same time." The doctor replied, "No problem. I will be glad to do both of them at once."

A week later, the two boys met again. The second little boy said to the first, "How was it having your tonsils taken out?" The first little boy replied, "I can tell you one thing. Your tonsils sure aren't where you think they are!"

15. How Do I Get There?

Boudreaux was frying fish and started a grease fire on the stove. He called the fire department and yelled excitedly, "This is Boudreaux. Y'all come quick. My house is on fire!"

The dispatcher tried to calm him down, "Take a deep breath, Mr. Boudreaux. How do we get there?"

Boudreaux paused for a moment, then asked, "Y'all ain't got that big red truck no more?"

16. I Got Here As Fast As I Could

The police officer got out of his car as the young man, stopped for speeding, rolled down his window.

"I've been waiting for you all day," the officer said, pulling out his notepad.

"Well, I got here as fast as I could," the young man replied.

17. Where Are You Calling From?

Fred Jones always read the obituary column. His friends knew his habit, so one day they decided to play a trick on him by placing his name and picture in the obituaries.

The following morning, Fred picked up his newspaper, turned to the obituary page, and there saw his name, biography, and photo. Startled, he immediately called his mother. "Mom, listen," he said. "Do you have the morning paper? You do? Please turn to the obituary page. You have? What did you see in the second column?"

There was a pause, and then his mother said, "My goodness! It's you, Fred! Listen, where are you calling from?"

18. Bragging Mistake

A man bought a ranch and was bragging to a friend about how large it was. "Why, I can get in my truck and start driving in the morning, and it is dark before I get to the other end of my property," he boasted. His friend, quite unimpressed, replied, "Yeah, I used to have a truck like that, too!"

19. I've Never Seen Anything Like That Before

A man was applying for a job at the railroad as a switchman and the interviewer said to him, "Sir, if you saw a train coming from one direction at 90 miles an hour and another train coming from the opposite direction at 90 miles an hour, and you knew they were going to collide and make a terrible wreck, what would you do?"

He replied, "I'd call my brother Henry."

The man said, "Call Henry? Why would you call Henry?"

He replied, "Because Henry ain't never seen a train wreck like that before."

20. I Got Here Early

The judge was in a merry mood on Christmas Eve as he asked the prisoner, "What are you charged with?"

"Doing my Christmas shopping early," replied the defendant.

"That's not an offense," said the judge. "How early were you doing this shopping?"

"Before the store opened."

21. A Day at the Zoo

"They were causing an awful lot of commotion at the zoo, your Honor," the zoo attendant said. "Boys," said the judge, "I never like to hear reports about juvenile delinquency. Now I want each of you to tell me your name and what you were doing wrong."

"My name is George," said the first boy, "and I threw peanuts into the elephant pen."

"My name is Larry," said the second boy, "and I threw peanuts into the elephant pen."

"My name is Mike," said the third boy, "and I threw peanuts into the elephant pen."

"My name is Peanuts," said the fourth boy.

22. He Tried It All

A man bought a parakeet, but after a week it hadn't spoken a word. So he went back to the pet shop to complain.

"Try getting him a mirror," the owner suggested. "They love to look at themselves. That will get him talking." The man bought the mirror, but the bird still refused to speak. A week later, the man went back to the pet store.

"Okay, try this bell," the owner advised. "The music will bring out the talker in him." A week later the man returned.

"He finally said something!" he told the store owner. "He looked in his mirror, rang his bell, said a few words, then dropped dead off his perch."

"Oh no!" the owner yelled. "What did he say?"

"He said, 'Doesn't that pet shop sell birdseed?'"

23. Feeling Your Importance

An arrogant army major had been promoted to Colonel. After he had inspected his new office and seated himself at the desk, an enlisted man knocked at the half-open door and started in. The colonel grabbed the phone, pausing long enough to say, "I'll be with you in a moment, Corporal." Continuing his phone conversation, the colonel said, "Yes, General. Thank you for calling. Yes, sir, I'll call the President immediately." Hanging up, the pompous Colonel turned to the waiting soldier, "What can I do for you, Corporal?"

"Nothing sir, I just came in to connect your phone."

24. Not a Problem

After joining the Navy, my husband underwent a physical. During the exam, it was discovered that, due to a bum shoulder, he couldn't fully extend his arms above his head. Perplexed, the doctor conferred with another physician. "Let him pass," said the second doctor. "I don't see any problems unless he has to surrender."

25. Losing Your Hair

There are three ways a man can wear his hair: parted, unparted, and departed.

26. What Were They Doing?

At a Hebrew school, Mr. Goldblatt, the new teacher, finished the lesson and asked if there were any questions. "Mr. Goldblatt," little Joey asked, "There is something I can't figure out."

"What is it Joey?"

"Well, according to the Bible, the children of Israel crossed the Red Sea, right?"

"Right."

"And the children of Israel beat up the Philistines right?"

"Well, in a manner of speaking, right."

"And the children of Israel built the temple, right?"

"Right."

"And the children of Israel fought the Egyptians and the Romans and were always doing something important, right?"

"All that is right, too," Mr. Goldblatt agreed.

"What then is your question?"

"What I want to know is this," said Joey, "What were all the grownups doing?"

27. Business is Business

One day at kindergarten, a teacher said to the class of 5-year olds, "I'll give $10 to the child who can tell me who was the most famous man who ever lived."

A little Irish boy put his hand up and said, "It was St. Patrick."

The teacher said, "Sorry, Sean, that's not correct."

Then a little Scottish boy put up his hand and said, "It was St. Andrew."

The teacher replied, "I'm sorry, Hamish, that's not right either."

Finally, a little Jewish boy raised his hand and said, "It was Jesus Christ."

The teacher said, "That's absolutely right, Marvin. Come up her and I'll give you the $10."

As the teacher was giving Marvin his money, she said, "You know, Marvin, since you're Jewish, I was very surprised you said, 'Jesus Christ.'"

Marvin replied, "Yeah, in my heart, I knew it was Moses, but business is business."

28. We Need to Go to Work

A bum asked a Jewish fellow, "Give me $10 till payday." The Jewish fellow responded, "When's payday?" The bum replied, "I don't know! You're the one that's working!"

29. That's the Guy I Want to See

A man owned a small ranch in Texas. The Texas Wage and Hour Department claimed he was not paying proper wages to his help and sent an agent out to interview him.

"I need a list of your employees and how much you pay them," demanded the agent.

"Well," replied the rancher, "There's my ranch hand who's been with me 3 years. I pay him $600 a week plus free room and board. The cook has been here 18 months and I pay her $500 a month plus free room and board. Then there's the half-wit who works about 18 hours every day and does about 90% of all the work around here. He makes about $10 per week, pays his own room and board, and gets T.V. privileges on Saturday nights."

"That's the guy I want to talk to, the half-wit," says the agent.

"That would be me," replied the rancher.

30. Exasperated

A woman was exasperated with her younger sister, who bought an unreliable car and called for a ride every time it broke down. One day, while out running errands, she received another call.

"What happened this time?" she asked.

"My brakes went out," her sister said. "Can you come and get me?"

"Where are you?"

"I'm in the drugstore."

"And where's the car?"

"It's in here with me."

31. Slander/Gossip

A woman who said to her friend, "My mother taught me never to say anything about anyone unless it was good. And boy is this good!"

32. Waiting for the Police

A woman and a man were involved in a car accident on a snowy, cold Monday morning. Both their cars were totally demolished, but amazingly neither of them were hurt.

After they crawled out of their car, the woman said, "Wow, just look at our cars! There is nothing left, but we are unhurt. This must be a sign from God that we should meet, be friends, and live together in peace for the rest of our days."

Flattered, the man replied, "O, yes, I agree with you completely, this must be a sign from God!"

The woman continued, "And look at this, here is another miracle, my car is completely demolished, but this bottle of wine did not break. Surely God wants us to drink this wine to celebrate our good fortune." Then she handed the bottle to the man.

The man nodded his head in agreement, opened it, drank half the bottle, and then handed it back to the woman. The woman took the bottle, immediately put the cork back in, and handed it back to the man.

The man asked, "Aren't you having any?"

The woman replied, "No. I think I'll just wait for the police."

33. Dad in Disguise

Two brothers were walking home from Sunday

School, each deep in his own thoughts. Finally, one boy said, "What do you think about all the devil stuff we learned today?"

The other replied thoughtfully, "Well, you know how Santa Claus turned out. The devil's probably just Dad in disguise, too."

34. "You Know You are a Redneck If . . ."

- You have at least one old refrigerator on your front porch.
- You can entertain yourself for more than 15 minutes with a fly swatter.
- Your boat has not left the driveway in 15 years.
- You burn your yard rather than mow it.
- The Salvation Army declines your furniture.
- You offer to give someone the shirt off your back and they don't want it.
- You have the local taxidermist on speed dial.
- You come back from the dump with more than you took.
- You keep a can of Raid on the kitchen table.
- You keep flea and tick soap in the shower.
- You've been involved in a custody fight over a hunting dog.
- You have a rag for a gas cap.
- Your house doesn't have curtains, but your truck does.
- You wonder how service stations keep their restrooms so clean.
- Your lifetime goal is to own a fireworks stand.
- You have a complete set of salad bowls and they all say "Cool Whip" on the side.

- Your working TV sits on top of your non-working TV.

- You've used your ironing board as a buffet table.

- You've used a toilet brush to scratch your back.

- You think fast food is hitting a deer at 65 mph.

35. You Know you're an East Texan if . . .

- Your richest relative buys a new house and you have to help take the wheels off.

- You think potted meat on a saltine is an hors d'oeuvre.

- There is a stuffed possum mounted in your home.

- You consider a bug-zapper quality entertainment.

- Directions to your house include "turn off the paved road."

- Your family tree does not fork.

- Your wife's hairdo has been ruined by a ceiling fan at least once.

- Your mother has ever been involved in a fistfight at a high school game.

- You've ever bar-be-cued Spam on the grill.

- You've ever worn a tube-top to a wedding.

- You think beef jerky and moon pies are two of the major food groups.

- You have more than two brothers named Bubba or Junior.

- Your father encourages you to quit school because Larry has an opening at the lube rack.

- You think the Styrofoam cooler is the greatest

invention of all time.

- You had a toothpick in your mouth when your wedding pictures were taken.

36. Why, Why, Why?

- Why do we press harder on a remote control when we knew the batteries are going dead?

- Why do banks charge a fee on "insufficient funds" when they know there is not enough money?

- Why does someone believe you when you say there are 4 billion stars, but check when you say the paint is wet?

- Why does Superman stop bullets with his chest, but ducks when you throw a revolver at him?

- If people evolved from apes, then why are there still apes?

- Is there ever a day that mattresses are not on sale?

- Why is it that no plastic bag will open from the end on your first try?

- How come you never hear father-in-law jokes?

- How do those dead bugs get into those enclosed light fixtures?

37. How About Them Cowboys?

A man died and went to heaven. St. Peter met him at the gate and asked, "What's your IQ?" The man replied, "170." St. Peter said, "Come on in. I want you to meet Albert Schweitzer. You two are going to have a wonderful time visiting together up here."

Another man came to the gate and St. Peter asked him, "What's your IQ?" He replied, "180." Peter said,

"Come on in. I want you to meet Albert Einstein. You two are going to enjoy one another. You can sit and talk about the theory of relativity all day long."

The next fellow walked up to the gate and St. Peter asked, "What's your IQ?" He replied, "70."

St. Peter then said, "How 'bout them Cowboys?"

38. Bumper Sticker

A man was being tailgated by a stressed-out woman on a busy boulevard.

Suddenly, the light turned yellow just in front of him. He did the right thing, stopping at the cross-walk, even though he could have beaten the red light by accelerating through the intersection. The tailgating woman was furious and honked her horn, screaming in frustration as she missed her chance to get through the intersection, dropping her cell phone and makeup. As she was still in mid-rant, she heard a tap on her window and looked up into the face of a very serious police officer. The officer ordered her to exit her car with her hands up. He took her to the police station where she was searched, finger printed, photographed, and placed in a holding cell. After a couple of hours, a policeman approached the cell and opened the door. She was escorted back to the booking desk and there the arresting officer was waiting with her personal effects. He said, "I'm very sorry for this mistake. You see, I pulled up behind your car while you were blowing your horn, shaking your fist at the guy in front of you, and cussing a blue streak at him. I noticed the 'What Would Jesus Do' bumper sticker, the 'Choose Life' license plate holder, the 'Follow Me to Sunday-School' bumper sticker, and the chrome-plated Christian fish emblem on the trunk. Naturally, I assumed you had stolen the car."

39. I Couldn't Find One

A group of Americans, retired teachers, recently went to France on a tour.

Robert Whiting, an elderly gentleman of 83, arrived in Paris by plane. At French customs, he took a few minutes to locate his passport in his carry-on. "You have been to France before monsieur?", the customs officer asked sarcastically. Mr. Whiting admitted that he had been to France previously.

"Then you should know enough to have your passport ready."

The American said, "The last time I was here I didn't have to show it."

"Impossible. Americans always have to show their passports on arrival in France!"

The American senior gave the Frenchman a long, hard look. The he quietly explained, "Well, when I came ashore at Omaha Beach on D-Day in 1944 to help liberate this country, I couldn't find any Frenchmen to show it to."

40. Where Did We Come From?

A little girl asked her mother, "How did the human race appear?"

The mother answered, "God made Adam and Eve and they had children and so was all mankind made."

Two days later she asked her father the same question. The father answered, "Many years ago there were monkeys from which the human race developed."

The confused girl went back to her mother and said, "Mom, how is it possible that you told me that the human race was created by God and Papa says they were developed from monkeys?"

The mother answered, "Well, dear, it is very simple. I told you about the origin of my side of the family and your father told you about his side."

Chapter 2

Preachers

1. Do You Know Who I Am?

A lady walked into church one Sunday and the usher met her at the door and asked, "Where would you like to be seated?" She replied, "Right on the front row." He responded, "Oh lady, you don't want to do that. Our preacher is the dullest preacher in the world."

She responded, "Do you know who I am?" He replied, "No, I don't." She said, "I am the preacher's mother."

The usher then asked, "Do you know who I am?" She replied, "No." He responded, "Good!"

2. Taking a Church Survey

A preacher said to a friend of his, "I'm going to take a survey in my church to find out what my members think I could do to make our church better."

His friend said, "Hey, that sounds like a good idea. Let me know how it turns out."

A few weeks later, the two met again and his friend said to him, "How did that survey turn out?"

He said, "Not so good. Their response was too vague. They didn't specify which lake . . . or what kind of kite."

3. Preacher Can't Preach

There was once a nasal tone singer who was such a poor singer that he was ruining the choir. Yet, he loved the choir and was one of its most faithful members. Finally, some of the members of the church came to the pastor and said, "You simply must do something about that singer. We can't stand his singing much longer." The pastor thought, "That man has a large family and many influential friends. If I dismiss him from the choir I'll be in trouble. I'll ask the chairman of the deacons to do it."

He asked the chairman and he responded, "Oh, pastor, you know I own a service station. That man has a large and influential family and they trade with from me. If I tell him he can't sing in the choir anymore, I'll lose all their business. I just can't do it."

Finally, the pastor decided he had to tackle the job by himself. So, he went to see George one night and said, "George, this is hard to say, but I must tell you. You must give up singing in the choir."

George was devastated. He said, "Why pastor? Why? That's the joy of my life!"

The pastor responded, "Well, George, just to tell you the truth, there are several people who said you can't sing."

George responded, "Oh, is that all? Pastor I've heard a whole lot more than that say you can't preach."

4. What Makes a Good Sermon

George Burns once said, "The secret of a good sermon is to have a good beginning and a good ending;

and to have the two as close together as possible."

5. Making the Wrong Choice

A Southern Baptist minister was completing a temperance sermon. With great emphasis he said, "If I had all the beer in the world, I'd take it and pour it into the river." With even greater emphasis he said, "And if I had all the wine in the world, I'd take it and pour it into the river." And then finally, shaking his fist in the air, he said, "And if I had all the whiskey in the world, I'd take it and pour it into the river."

When the sermon was complete, he sat down. The song leader stood and announced, "For our closing song, let us sing Hymn 365, "Shall We Gather at the River.""

6. Sleep – A Comment

The young pastor heard that his distinguished and very literary father-in-law was coming to town for a couple of weeks. The ambitious young man asked his father-in-law to do him a favor and provide helpful criticism for his sermons. "All I ask for is an honest opinion," he said. The first Sunday came and the young pastor was appalled to see his father-in-law going to sleep in the middle of his sermon. The next Sunday the same thing happened. "I had asked you to give me your opinion of my sermons," the young pastor said to his departing company, "but I know that would be difficult since you slept through both of them." "Young man," the distinguished gentleman responded, "Sleep IS an opinion."

7. You're Something Else

A new preacher came to town and people walked by to greet him after the sermon. One lady came out and said, "You are something else." The next Sunday, she did the same thing, and the next again. Time after time, she would stop and say, "You are something else."

He began to wonder what she meant by that. So one day, he asked one of his deacons if he knew. The deacon said he didn't but suggested that the preacher ask the lady what she meant.

So the next Sunday, she walked out and said, "You are something else." He said, "I've heard you say that many times. What do you mean by it?" She replied, "You must be something else, because you're sure not much of a preacher."

8. We Are but Dust

A visiting minister during the offertory prayer:

"Dear Lord," he began with arms extended and a rapturous look on his upturned face, "without you we are but dust . . ."

He would have continued, but at that moment one very obedient little girl leaned over to her mother and asked quite audibly in her shrill little girl voice, "Mommy what is BUTT dust?"

9. Watch Yourself

A preacher went to visit one of his parishioners, and as he stood by the bedside, the man began to gasp and motioned for the preacher to hand him a pencil and a piece of paper which is what he did. He assumed that the man wanted to write something important. Just as he finished, the man gave one last gasp and died. The preacher folded the note up, put it in his pocket, and assumed that it was something that he would want remembered as his last words. He decided to leave the note in his pocket until the funeral service and then take it out and read it to the congregation so that they could hear the man's last parting wish.

The time came for the service and the preacher walked out on the platform. Remembering the note, he reached in his pocket and pulled it out and read, "You are standing on my oxygen tube."

10. It's a Preacher's Duty

A preacher went to his church on Monday morning and discovered a dead mule in the church yard. He called the police. Since there did not appear to be any foul play, the police referred the preacher to the health department. They said since there was no health threat that he should call the sanitation department.

The sanitation manager said he could not pick up the mule without authorization from the mayor. Now the preacher knew the mayor and was not eager to call him. The mayor had a bad temper and was generally hard to deal with, but the preacher called him anyway.

The mayor did not disappoint him. He immediately began to rant and rave at the pastor and finally said, "Why did you call me anyway? Isn't it your job to bury the dead?"

The preacher paused for a brief prayer and asked the Lord to direct his response. He was led to say, "Yes, Mayor, it is my job to bury the dead, but I always like to notify the next of kin first."

11. Young Preacher's First Funeral

As a young minister, who had never conducted a funeral I was asked by a funeral director to hold a graveside service for a homeless man, with no family or friends, who had died while traveling through the area. The funeral was to be held at a cemetery way back in the country, and this man would be the first to be laid to rest there.

As I was not familiar with the backwoods area, I became lost, and being a typical man, I did not stop for directions. I finally arrived an hour late. I saw the crew eating lunch, but the hearse was nowhere in sight. I apologized to the workers for my tardiness, and stepped to the side of the open grave, where I saw the vault lid already in place. I assured the workers I would not hold them long, but this was the proper thing to do.

The workers gathered around, still eating their lunch. I poured out my heart and soul. As I preached, the workers began to say, "Amen," "Praise the Lord," and "Glory!" I preached and I preached, like I'd never preached before, from Genesis all the way to Revelation.

I closed the lengthy service with a prayer and walked to my car. I felt I had done my duty for the homeless man and that the crew would leave with a renewed sense of purpose and dedication, in spite of my tardiness.

As I was opening the door and taking off my coat, I overheard one of the workers saying to another, "I ain't never seen anything like this before . . . and I've been putting in septic tanks for twenty years."

Chapter 3

Marriage

1. Marriage – Anniversary

My wife and I recently celebrated our fifty-third wedding anniversary.

The week before, I said to her, "Honey, did you ever imagine in your wildest dreams that you would be married to me for fifty-three years?"

She replied, "Paul, you were never a part of my wildest dreams."

2. It Costs Too Much

A man said to his wife, "What would you like for your anniversary?" She said, "I want a divorce." He said, "I wasn't thinking of spending that much."

3. One For All Occasions

A lady went to her college reunion and people asked how things were going. She said, "I have been married four times and all four of my husbands died." They responded, "Wow! Four times? Who did you marry?" She said, "I married a banker, an actor, a preacher, and an undertaker, in that order." They said, "That's a strange order, isn't it?" She said, "Yes, but I married them: one for the money, two for the show, three to get ready, and four to go."

4. Everything Is in My Name

A lady was milling around in the cathedral of a fine cemetery, and the caretaker became concerned and went over to her and asked her if he could help. She said, "I'm looking for the grave of my late husband, Carl Thornton." He said, "Well, come to my office and we'll look it up in the books and locate it for you." So they went to his office and looked through the books and he finally said, "I'm sorry, but there is no Carl Thornton here. I do, however, have a Nita Thornton." She said, "That's it, everything is in my name."

5. Credit Card Stolen

A man said, "Someone stole all my credit cards, but I won't be reporting it. The thief spends less than my wife did."

6. Rest in Peace

After 50 years of marriage the husband died. His wife had him buried under a headstone that read, "MAY HE REST IN PEACE." When the man's will was probated, the wife found that he had left most of his estate to his young secretary. The wife made a trip to the cemetery to ask if she could have a phrase added to her late husband's headstone. The director of the cemetery said he would be glad to do it. He asked what to add. The wife replied, "TILL WE MEET AGAIN."

7. Children

The census taker introduced himself to a woman who was working in her yard and asked if he could interview her.

She agreed to be interviewed and led the man inside. He started with a few demographic questions, and then moved on to her family.

"So, how many children do you and your husband have?" he asked.

"Four. Eenie, Meenie, Minie, and George."

"What?" the census taker replied, amused. "Why'd you name your fourth child George?"

"Because we didn't want any Moe."

8. Talk to Your Wife

An insurance salesman tried to persuade a housewife that she should take out life insurance. "Suppose your husband were to die," he said. "What would you get?"

The housewife thought for a while and then said, "Oh, a parrot, I think. Then the house wouldn't seem so quiet."

9. Remember Your Anniversary

A husband was in big trouble when he forgot his wedding anniversary.

His wife told him, "Tomorrow there better be something in the driveway for me that goes from 0 to 200 in 2 seconds flat."

The next morning the wife found a small package in the driveway. She opened it and found a brand new bathroom scale. Funeral arrangements for the husband have been set for Saturday.

10. A Good Woman Is Hard to Find

Two guys from Benson County are quietly sitting in a boat at Devils Lake, North Dakota, fishing and sucking down beer when suddenly Mel says, "I think I'm going to divorce my wife – she hasn't spoken to me in over 2 months."

Earl sips his beer and says, "You better think it over – good women like that are hard to find."

11. Talk To One Another

A man said, "My wife and I had words, but I didn't get to use mine."

12. Visit His Grave

An elderly man decided to make a will. He told his lawyer he had two final requests. First, he wanted to be cremated and second, he wanted the ashes scattered over Wal-Mart. The lawyer asked, "Why Wal-Mart?"

"Because I'll be sure my wife will visit me at least twice a week."

13. Better Tell the Truth

A man calls home to his wife and says, "Honey, I have been asked to go fishing up in Canada with my boss and several of his friends. We'll be gone for a week. This is a good opportunity for me to get that promotion I've been wanting so could you please pack enough clothes for a week and set out my rod and tackle box? We're leaving from the office and I will swing by the house to pick my things up. Oh! Please pack my new blue silk pajamas."

The wife thinks this sounds a bit fishy, but being the good wife she does exactly what her husband asked. The following weekend he came home a little tired but otherwise looking good. The wife welcomes him home and asks if he caught many fish.

He says, "Yes! Lots of Walleye, some Blue gill, and a few Pike. But why didn't you pack my new blue silk pajamas like I asked you to do?"

The wife replies, "I did. They're in your tackle box."

14. Wife Keeping Yourself Attractive

A woman was walking down the street when she was accosted by a particularly dirty and shabby-looking homeless woman who asked me for a couple of dollars for dinner. She took out her wallet, got out ten dollars and asked, "If I give you this money, will you buy some wine with it instead of dinner?"

"No, I had to stop drinking years ago," the homeless woman told her.

"Will you use it to go shopping instead of buying food?" she asked.

"No way! I need to spend all my time trying to stay alive," replied the woman.

"Will you spend this on a beauty salon instead of food?" she asked.

"Are you nuts? I haven't had my hair done in 20 years!"

"Well," she said, "I'm not going to give you the money. Instead, I'm going to take you out for dinner with my husband and me tonight." The homeless woman was shocked.

"Won't your husband be furious with you for doing that? I know I'm dirty, and I probably smell pretty disgusting."

I said, "That's okay. It's important for him to see what a woman looks like after she has given up shopping, hair appointments, and wine."

15. Write a Check

A man who was filthy rich was on his deathbed and he said to his wife, "I've heard all of my life, 'you can't take it with you,' but I want to try. So, when I die, I want you to take all of my millions, put them in a cigar box, put the cigar box in the casket and let me take it with me."

She was aghast. She said, "What about me and the kids?" He said, "Well, I have set up a trust fund that will pay you about $50,000 a year. That should be sufficient."

When she told her son what her husband had requested, he said, "Mom, surely you didn't put all of those millions in that casket with Dad, did you?" She said, "Well, I did exactly what he requested. When he died, I went down to the bank and withdrew all of his millions of dollars and put them in my account. Then I wrote a personal check for $10 million, put it in the cigar box, and put it in the casket."

16. The Silent Treatment

A husband and wife were experiencing some problems in their relationship at home. It got to the point where they began to give each other "the silent treatment." Neither said a word to the other all evening. Suddenly the man realized that the next day he needed his wife to wake him up early for a business flight. Not wanting to be the first to break the silence, he wrote on a piece of paper, "Wake me up at 5 a.m." He left it where he knew she would see it and then went to bed.

The next morning the husband woke up, only to discover it was 9 a.m. and he had missed his plane. Angry, he was ready to find his wife and learn why she had not woken him up. Suddenly he noticed a note beside the bed. It was from his wife. The note said, "It's 5 a.m. Wake up."

17. Bad Choices

The woman applying for a job in a Florida lemon grove seemed way too qualified for the job. "Look, miss," said the foreman, "have you any actual experience in picking lemons?"

"Well, as a matter of fact, yes!" she replied. "I've been divorced three times."

18. Anniversary Trip

With a man soon to celebrate his 50th wedding anniversary at the church's marriage marathon, the minister asked Pete to take a few minutes and share some insight into how he managed to maintain his marriage with the same woman all these years.

The husband replied to the audience, "Well, I treated her with respect, spent money on her, but mostly I took her traveling on special occasions."

The minister inquired, "Trips to where?"

"For our 25th anniversary, I took her to Beijing,

China."

The minister then said, "What a terrific example you are to all husbands, Pete. Please tell the audience what you're going to do for your wife on your 50th anniversary."

"I'm going back to get her."

19. Learn to Compliment Your Wife

A woman, standing nude, looks in the bedroom mirror and says to her husband, "I look horrible. I feel fat and ugly. Pay me a compliment." The husband replies, "Your eyesight's near perfect."

20. I Married Your Sister

Leena was tired of her husband coming home drunk, and decided to scare him straight. One night, she put on a devil costume and hid behind a tree to intercept him on the way home. When her husband walked by, she jumped out and stood before him with her red horns, long tail and pitchfork.

"Who are you?" he slurred.

"I'm the devil," she answered.

"Well, come on home with me," he said. "I married your sister."

21. Lost Wife

Two old guys are pushing their carts around Wal-Mart when they collide.

The first old guy says to the second guy, "Sorry about that. I'm looking for my wife, and I guess I wasn't paying attention to where I was going."

The second old guy says, "That's OK. It's a coincidence. I'm looking for my wife too, and I can't find her and I'm getting a little desperate."

The first old guy says, "Well, maybe I can help you find her. What does she look like?"

The second old guy says, "Well, she is 27 years old, tall with red hair, blue eyes, long legs, wearing short shorts. What does your wife look like?"

To which the first old guy says, "Never mind my wife; let's look for yours."

22. A Memorial Stone

A woman's husband dies. He had $30,000 in the bank. After everything is done at the funeral home and cemetery, she tells her closest friend that there is none of the $30,000 left. The friend says, "How can that be?" The woman replies, "Well, the funeral cost me $6,500. And of course I made a donation to the church. That was $500, and I spent another $500 for the wake, food and drinks, you know ... The rest went for the memorial stone." The friend says, "$22,500 for the memorial stone? My God, how big is it?" The woman held out her finger and said, "Three Carats!"

23. It's a Sign

Spotted near a Salt Lake City courthouse: "Love is grand. Divorce is 50 grand."

24. Wisdom of an Elderly Woman

Sally was driving home from one of her business trips in Northern Arizona when she saw an elderly Navajo woman walking on the side of the road. As the trip was a long and quiet one, she stopped the car and asked the Navajo woman if she would like a ride. With a silent nod of thanks, the woman got into the car.

Resuming the journey, Sally tried in vain to make a bit of small talk with the Navajo woman. The old woman just sat silently looking intently at everything she saw, studying every little detail, until she noticed a brown bag on the seat next to Sally. Sally looked down at the brown bag and said, "It's a bottle of wine. I got it for my husband."

The Navajo woman was silent for a moment or two. Then speaking with the quiet wisdom of an elder, she said, "Good trade."

25. Listen Carefully

A man was sitting on the edge of the bed, observing his wife looking at herself in the mirror. Since her birthday was not far off, he asked what she'd like to have for her birthday.

"I'd like to be six again," she replied, still looking in the mirror.

On the morning of her birthday, he arose early, made her a big bowl of Lucky Charms, and then took her to Six Flags. They rode every ride in the park: The Death Slide, Wall of Fear, Texas Giant, everything that was there.

Five hours later, they staggered out of the theme park. Her head was reeling and her stomach felt upside down. He then took her to McDonald's where he ordered her a Happy Meal with extra fries and a chocolate shake. Then it was off to a movie, popcorn, a soda pop, and her favorite candy, M&M's.

Finally, she wobbled home with her husband and collapsed into bed exhausted. He leaned over his wife with a big smile and lovingly asked, "Well, dear, what was it like being six again?"

"I meant my dress size, you moron!"

26. You're Bad Luck

A woman's husband had been slipping in and out of a coma for several months, yet she had stayed by his bedside every single day. One day, when he came to, he motioned for her to come nearer. As she sat by him, he whispered, eyes filled with tears, "Bessie, you know what? You have been with me all through the bad times. When I got fired, you were there to support me. When my business failed, you were there. When I got shot, you were by my side. When we lost the house, you stayed right here."

"What dear?" she gently asked smiling as her heart began to be filled with warmth.

"Bessie, I think you are bad luck . . ."

27. Older Women

After being married for 44 years, I took a careful look at my wife one day and said, "Honey, 44 years ago we had a cheap apartment, a cheap car, slept on a sofa bed and watched a 10-inch black-and-white TV, but I got to sleep every night with a hot 25-year-old gal. Now I have a $500,000 house, a $45,000 car, nice big bed and a plasma screen TV, but I'm sleeping with a 69-year-old woman. It seems to me that you're not holding up your side of things."

My wife is a very reasonable woman. She told me to go out and find a hot 25-year-old gal, and she would make sure that I would once again be living in a cheap apartment, driving a cheap car, sleeping on a sofa bed and watching a 10-inch black-and-white TV.

Aren't older women great? They really know how to solve your problems.

Chapter 4

Age

1. But I'm Still Driving

I visited a dear lady in a nursing home recently, and asked how she was doing. She said, "Pastor, I've got cataracts and I am nearly blind, paralyzed on my left side, and have almost lost my hearing, but thank God I can still drive."

2. Slapped Three Times

An 80-year-old-woman who was living with her daughter had a date one night with a 90-year-old-man. This was the first date she had had in years, and her daughter was worried about her. She said to her, "Momma, you two be careful, and you be home by 10:00 sharp or I'll be worried about you." The mother promised.

Ten-o'clock came, and the mother was not home. Eleven o'clock came, and she was still not there. Her daughter was walking the floor, worried to death. When her mother finally arrived at 11:15, she said, "Mother, where in the world have you been?" Her mother responded, "We went to a movie and then to a drive-in, but I had to slap him three times."

Her daughter said, "You mean, he got fresh with you?" The mother replied, "No, to see if he was still alive."

3. How Do You Feel?

Two elderly gentlemen from a retirement center were sitting on a bench under a tree when one turns to the other and says, "Slim, I'm 83 years old now and I'm just full of aches and pains. I know you're about my age. How do you feel?"

Slim says, "I feel just like a new-born baby."

"Really? Like a new-born baby?

"Yep. No hair, no teeth, and I think I just wet my pants."

4. Hearing Changed My Will

An elderly gentleman had serious hearing problems for a number of years.

He went to the doctor and the doctor was able to have him fitted for a set of hearing aids that allowed the gentleman to hear 100%.

The elderly gentleman went back in a month to the doctor and the doctor said, "Your hearing is perfect. Your family must be really pleased that you can hear again."

The gentleman replied, "Oh, I haven't told my family yet. I just sit around, listen to the conversations, and I've changed my will three times!"

5. Memory

A very elderly gentleman (mid-nineties), very well dressed, hair well groomed, great-looking suit, flower in his lapel smelling slightly of a good after shave, presenting a well-looked image, walks into an upscale cocktail lounge. Seated at the bar is an elderly looking lady in her mid-fifties. The gentleman walks over, sits alongside of her, orders a drink, takes a sip, turns to her and says, "So tell me, do I come here often?"

6. Hard of Hearing

An old man and an old lady were sitting before the fire one cold winter's evening. The old man had never been very demonstrative, but his heart welled up within him as he thought about his wife, so he mustered up some courage and said to her, "I am proud of you."

She was hard of hearing, and so she said, "What did you say?" And he responded again, "I am proud of you." She once again said even louder, "What did you say?" He said, "I am proud of you." Then she asked a third time really loudly, "What did you say?" And he yelled out to her, "I am proud of you." And she responded, "Yes, and I'm tired of you, too."

7. Memory – Better Write It Down

An old man and old lady were losing their memory, and someone told him that they should learn to write things down. So they were sitting on the front porch in the rocking chair one cool summer evening and he said to her, "You know what I'd like to have?" She said, "No, what?" He said, "I'd like to have some ice cream with chocolate syrup on the top." She said, "Well, I'll go get it for you." He said, "You'd better write it down."

She responded, "No, I can remember that." In about thirty minutes, she came back with some scrambled eggs and bacon. He responded, "I told you to write it down. You forgot the toast."

8. Eyesight

A faithful parishioner came to talk to her pastor about a serious spiritual problem. "I have sinned in my life, pastor," she confessed. "What is it, Mrs. Jones?"

"It's vanity," she replied. "You know that large mirror in the foyer? Everybody stops there on the way into church to check their hair or straighten their tie, but when I look in the mirror, I linger. I look at myself and I can't resist saying, 'You are one gorgeous woman!'"

The pastor broke it in, "Oh, Mrs. Jones," he said, "That's not vanity; you've just got cataracts."

9. Driving the Wrong Way

An old man was driving down the freeway when his cell phone rang. It was his wife. "Dear," she said, "I just heard on the radio that a car is going the wrong way on your highway. Please be careful!"

"It's not just one car, there are hundreds of them!" he replied.

10. We Can't Wait Long

Because they had no reservations at a busy restaurant, my elderly neighbor and his wife were told there would be a 45-minute wait for a table. "Young man, we're both 90 years old," the husband said. "We may not have 45 minutes."

They were seated immediately.

11. Eat Right

An old man and his wife, both 85, were involved in

an automobile accident and died and went to heaven. Both of them had exercised their whole lives, eaten right, and taken care of themselves, but suddenly they found themselves in heaven as a result of the accident. St. Peter showed them around a beautiful mansion, swimming pool, Jacuzzi, and all of that. The man asked, "What is this going to cost?" St. Peter said, "You don't understand. This is heaven." Then he looked out the window and said, "There is a beautiful golf course where you can play every day, and the course changes continually so that you will have new experiences." The man said, "That's wonderful! How much is it going to cost?" St. Peter said, "You don't understand. This is heaven." Then he took them to the club house and showed them all the food they had to eat, and the man said, "Oh my goodness, this is wonderful! But what about the light food, the cholesterol-free food?" St. Peter said, "You don't get it. This is heaven. You don't worry about health foods and cholesterol up here in heaven." With that, the old man took off his hat, threw it on the ground, and began to stomp on it, and St. Peter said, "What's the matter?" The man turned to his wife and said, "If it hadn't been for those blasted bran muffins you've been giving me, I could have been here ten years sooner."

12. Anniversary Wish

A man and his wife, now in their 60's, were celebrating their 40th wedding anniversary. On their special day a good fairy came to them and said that because they had been so good that each one of them could have one wish. The wife wished for a trip around the world with her husband. Whoosh! Immediately she had airline/cruise tickets in her hands. The man wished for a female companion 30 years younger. Whoosh . . . immediately he turned ninety!!!

13. Memory

An elderly couple had dinner at another couple's house, and after eating, the wives left the table and went into the kitchen. The two gentlemen were talking, and one said, "Last night we went out to a new restaurant and it was really great. I would recommend it very highly." The other man said, "What is the name of the restaurant?"

The first man thought and thought and finally said, "What is the name of the flower you give to someone you love? You know . . . the one that's red and has thorns."

"Do you mean a rose?"

"Yes, that's the one," replied the man. He then turned towards the kitchen and yelled, "Rose, what's the name of that restaurant we went to last night?"

14. You Might Die

An old gentleman was getting a physical before marrying a young woman.

The doctor asked admiringly, "How old are you, sir?" The old gentleman replied, "Eighty-seven." The doctor asked, "And the bride?" The old fellow said, "She's 23." The doctor predicted, "That kind of disparity in your ages could be fatal." The old gentleman shrugged, "If she dies, she dies."

15. Birthday Celebration

"Look at me!" the fit old man boasted to a group of young people. "Fit as a fiddle! And you want to know why? I don't smoke, I don't drink, I don't stay up late, and I don't chase women." He smiled at them, "And tomorrow I'm going to celebrate my 90th birthday."

"Oh really?" drawled a young man. "How?"

16. While You're There

While on a road trip, an elderly couple stopped at a roadside restaurant for lunch. After finishing their meal, they left the restaurant and resumed their trip. When leaving, the elderly woman unknowingly left her glasses on the table and she didn't miss them until after they had been driving about twenty minutes. By then, to add to the aggravation, they had to travel quite a distance before they could find a place to turn around in order to return to the restaurant to retrieve her glasses. All the way back, the elderly husband became the classic grouchy old man. He fussed and complained and scolded his wife relentlessly during the entire return drive. The more he chided her, the more agitated he became. He just wouldn't let up one minute.

To her relief they finally arrived at the restaurant. As the woman got out of the car and hurried inside to retrieve her glasses, the old Geezer yelled to her . . . "While you're in there, you might as well get my hat and the credit card."

17. I Forgot the Tickets

An old man and his wife were standing in a long

line at the ticket counter in an airport. The old man turned to his wife and said, "I sure wish we had brought the piano with us." She said, "What do you mean? We've got 16 bags." He said, "Yes, but the tickets are on the piano."

18. Senior Breakfast

A couple went to breakfast at a restaurant where the "Senior's Special" was two eggs, bacon, hash browns and toast for $1.99.

"Sounds good," the wife said. "But I don't want any eggs."

"Then I'll have to charge you two dollars and forty-nine cents because you're ordering a la carte," the waitress warned her.

"You mean I'd have to pay for not taking the eggs?" she asked.

"Yes."

"I'll take the special."

"How do you want your eggs?"

"Raw and in the shell," she replied. She took the two eggs home.

19. God's Getting Better

A little girl was sitting on her grandfather's lap as he read her a bedtime story. From time to time, she would take her eyes off the book and reach up to touch his wrinkled cheek. She was alternately stroking her own cheek, then his again.

Finally she spoke up, "Grandpa, did God make you?"

"Yes, sweetheart," he answered, "God made me a long time ago."

"Oh," she paused, "Grandpa, did God make me, too?"

"Yes, indeed, honey," he said, "God made you just a little while ago."

Feeling their respective faces again, she observed, "God's getting better at it, isn't he?"

20. Make 'em Good

An elderly Florida lady did her shopping and, upon returning to her car, found four males in the act of leaving with her vehicle. She dropped her shopping bags and drew her hand gun, proceeding to scream at the top of her lungs, "I have a gun and I know how to use it! Get out of the car!" The poor men didn't wait for a second threat. They got out and ran like mad.

The lady, somewhat shaken, then proceeded to load her shopping bags into the back seat of the car and got into the driver seat. She was so shaken that she could not get her key in the ignition.

She tried and tried, and then she realized why. It was for the same reason that she wondered why there was a football, a Frisbee, and two twelve-packs of beer in the front seat. A few minutes later she found her own car parked four or five spaces further down. She loaded her bags into the car and drove to the police station to report her mistake.

The sergeant to whom she told the story could not stop laughing. He pointed to the other end of the counter where four pale men were reporting a car jacking by a mad, elderly woman described as white, less than five feet tall, glasses and clearly white hair and carrying a large hand gun.

No charges were filed.

21. When Grandpa Croaks

A six-year-old goes to the hospital with his grandma to visit his grandpa.

When they get to the hospital, he runs ahead of his grandma and bursts into his grandpa's room.

"Grandpa, Grandpa," he says excitedly, "as soon as Grandma comes into the room, make a noise like a frog!"

"What?" said his grandpa.

"Make a noise like a frog because grandma said that as soon as you croak, we're going to Disneyland!!"

22. The Class is Over

I feel like my body has gotten totally out of shape, so I got my doctor's permission to join a fitness club and start exercising. I decided to take an aerobics class for seniors. I bent, twisted, gyrated, jumped up and down, and perspired for an hour. But, by the time I got my leotards on, the class was over.

23. No Peer Pressure

Reporters interviewing a 104-year-old woman: "And what do you think is the best thing about being 104?" the reporter asked. She simply replied, "No peer pressure."

24. No Need to Go Home

Just before the funeral services, the undertaker

came up to the very elderly widow and asked, "How old was your husband?"

"98," she replied. "Two years older than me."

"So you're 96," the undertaker commented.

She responded, "Hardly worth going home, is it?"

Chapter 5

Doctors

1. Pay Your Bills

The doctor gave a man six months to live. The man couldn't pay his bill, so the doctor gave him another six months.

2. Your Check Came Back

The doctor called Mrs. Cohen saying, "Mrs. Cohen, your check came back." Mrs. Cohen answered, "So did my arthritis!"

3. The Right Diagnosis

Doctor: "You'll live to be 75."
Patient: "I am 75!"
Doctor: "See! What did I tell you?"

4. I've Got Shingles

Bubba walks in and the receptionist asked him what he had. Bubba said, "Shingles." So she wrote down his name, address, insurance info, and told him to have a seat.

Fifteen minutes later a nurse's aide came out and asked Bubba what he had. Bubba said, "Shingles." So she recorded his weight, height, and assorted medical history and told Bubba to wait in the examining room.

A half hour later a nurse came and asked Bubba

what he had. Bubba said, "Shingles." So the nurse gave Bubba a blood test, an electrocardiogram, and told Bubba to take off all his clothes and wait for the doctor.

An hour later the doctor came in and asked what he had. Bubba said, "Shingles." The doctor asked, "Where?" Bubba said, "Outside on the delivery truck. Where do you want me to put them?"

5. The Right Prescription

An elderly lady, obviously upset, called her doctor. "Is it true," she asked, "that the medicine you prescribed will have to be taken for the rest of my life?"

"Yes, I'm afraid so," said the doctor.

"I'm just wondering then just how serious my condition is because this prescription is marked NO REFILLS!"

6. Follow the Hospital Rules

Hospital regulations require a wheelchair for patients being discharged.

However, while working as a student nurse, a young nurse found one elderly gentleman - - already dressed and sitting on the bed with a suitcase at his feet - - who insisted he didn't need my help to leave the hospital.

After a chat about rules being rules, he reluctantly let her wheel him to the elevator. On the way down she asked him if his wife was meeting him. "I don't know," he said. "She's still upstairs in the bathroom changing out of her hospital gown."

7. Are You Normal?

During a visit to the mental asylum, a visitor asked the director what the criterion was which defined whether or not a patient should be institutionalized.

"Well," said the director, "we fill up a bathtub, then we offer a teaspoon, a teacup and a bucket to the patient and ask him or her to empty the bathtub."

"Oh, I understand," said the visitor. "A normal person would use the bucket because it's bigger than the spoon or the teacup."

Now which one did you chose? Don't strain your brain, it's not that hard of a question. Let's see what the director said:

"No," said the director. "A normal person would pull the plug. Now do you want a bed near the window?"

Chapter 6

Finance

1. Rewards

A pastor said to his congregation, "We are taking a special collection for our building fund today and the person who makes the largest contribution is going to be allowed to pick the hymns." They passed the collection plate, and a nice-looking middle-aged lady dropped a $1,000 check in the collection plate.

When a pastor saw the large check, he called the lady by name and invited her to the front. He said, My dear, you have made the largest contribution today, so you get to pick three hymns." She looked out across the congregation and pointed to three different men saying, "I'll take him, and him, and him."

2. They Will Find you

Two men were shipwrecked on an island. The minute they made it to shore, one of them started screaming and yelling. "We're going to die! There's no food, no water! We're going to die!"

The second man propped himself against a palm tree and seemed so calm, the first man felt he was going crazy. "Don't you understand?" he yelled. "We're going to die!"

"You don't understand. I made a $100,000 pledge to our new church building fund," the second man said.

"What difference does that make? We're on an island with no food and no water."

"My pastor will find me."

3. Your Money's Worth

After church one Sunday morning, a mother commented, "The choir was awful this morning." The father commented, "The sermon was too long." Their 7-year-old daughter added, "But, you've got to admit it was a pretty good show for just a dollar."

4. The Chip Monk

I heard that in Las Vegas sometimes people put their poker chips in the collection plate. Believe it or not, the churches all receive these in their offerings—the Baptists, Methodists, Presbyterians, Catholics, all of them. Some of the churches felt a little uneasy taking their poker chips down to the casinos to cash them in, and so they all got together and hired a Franciscan monk to cash in their chips for them. He was called "the chip monk."

5. Estate Planning

When Dan found out he was going to inherit a fortune when his sickly father died, he decided he needed a woman to enjoy it with. So, one evening he went to a single's bar where he spotted the most beautiful woman he had ever seen. Her natural beauty took his breath away.

"I may look like an ordinary man," he said, "But in a just a few months, my father will die, and I will inherit 20 million dollars." Impressed, the woman went home with him that evening, and three days later, she became his stepmother.

6. Porky

A man called the church office one day and said to the secretary, "I'd like to speak to the top hog at the trough." The secretary was incensed and said to the man, "Sir, I'll have you know that we don't refer to our pastor as a hog." The man replied, "I'm sorry, I meant no offense. I just wanted to tell him I was going to write out a check for $10,000 for the church." The secretary replied, "Oh, hold on just a minute. I think I see the big pig coming in the office right now."

Chapter 7

Death

1. You Need to Be Ready

Two 90- year-old men, Moe and Joe, have been friends all of their lives.

When it's clear that Joe is dying, Moe visits him every day. One day Moe says, "Joe, we both loved baseball all our lives, and we played minor league ball together for so many years. Please do me one favor: when you get to Heaven, somehow you must let me know if there's baseball there."

Joe looks up at Moe from his deathbed, "Moe, you've been my best friend for many years. If it's at all possible, I'll do this favor for you." Shortly after that, Joe passes on. At midnight a couple of nights later, Moe is awakened from a sound sleep by a blinding flash of white light and a voice calling out to him, "Moe, Moe."

"Who is it," asks Moe, sitting up suddenly.

"Moe – it's me, Joe."

"You're not Joe. Joe just died."

"I'm telling you, it's me, Joe," insists the voice.

"Joe! Where are you?"

"In Heaven," replies Joe. "I have some really good news and a little bad news."

"Tell me the good news first," says Moe.

"The good news," Joe says, "is that there's baseball in Heaven. Better yet, all of our old buddies who died before us are here, too. Better than that, we're all young again. Better still, it's always springtime, and it never rains or snows. And best of all, we can play baseball all we want, and we never get tired."

"That's fantastic," says Moe. "It's beyond my wildest dreams! So what's the bad news?"

"You're pitching Tuesday."

2. She Made it There

As with many funerals, it was a cloudy, rainy day. The deceased was a little old lady who had devoted her entire married life to nagging her poor husband. When the graveside service had no more than ended, there was a tremendous lighting bolt accompanied by a burst of thunder and more rumbling thunder. The little old man looked at the pastor and calmly said, "Well, she's there."

3. How to Break the News

A man had a cat he loved very dearly and was going to make a trip to Italy. Before he left, he entrusted the cat to a friend. After about the third day on the trip, he called his friend to ask how the cat was doing. The friend said, "I hate to tell you this, but the cat died."

Needless to say, the man was devastated. He called back the next day, "Friend, you were brutal in the way you broke the news to me about my cat. You know how much I love that cat. Surely you could have been more diplomatic in telling me how the cat died."

The friend said, "Well, what do you suggest?"

"You could have told me on the first day, 'The cat's up on the roof and we're trying to get her down.' Then when I called back the second day, you could have said, 'Well, the cat fell and we took her to the vet, and the vet is trying to help her.' When I called back on the third day, you could have told me the cat died. That way, you would have broken the news gradually. By the way, how's mother?"

The man replied, "She's up on the roof."

4. What Would You Like For Them to Say?

Three friends from the local congregation were asked, "When you're in your casket, and friends and congregation members are mourning over you, what would you like them to say?"

Artie said, "I would like them to say I was a wonderful husband, a fine spiritual leader, and a great family man." Eugene commented, "I would like them to say I was a wonderful teacher and servant of God who make a huge difference in people's lives." Al said, "I'd like them to say, 'Look, he's moving!'"

5. Get Ready Early

An elderly Italian man lay dying in his bed. While suffering the agonies of impending death, he suddenly smelled the aroma of his favorite Italian anisette sprinkle cookies wafting up the stairs. He gathered his remaining strength, and lifted himself from the bed. Leaning against the wall, he slowly made his way out of the bedroom, and with even greater effort, gripping the railing with both hands, he crawled downstairs. With labored breath, he leaned against the door frame, gazing into the kitchen.

Were if not for death's agony, he would have himself already in heaven, for there, spread out upon waxed paper on the kitchen table were literally hundreds of his favorite anisette sprinkled cookies. Was it heaven? Or was it one final act of heroic love from his devoted Italian wife of sixty years, seeing to it that he left this world a happy man?

Mustering one great final effort, he threw himself towards the table, landing on his knees in a crumpled posture. His parched lips parted, the wondrous taste of the cookie was already in his mouth, seemingly bringing him back to life. The aged and withered hand trembled on its way to a cookie at the edge of the table, when it was suddenly smacked with a spatula by his wife . . .

"Back off!" she said, "They're for the funeral."

Chapter 8

Religion

1. What to Do About Baptists

I was in a local restaurant in a small West Texas town having breakfast one morning when I overheard two of the local ranchers talking. Apparently there had been some conflict in the community and Baptists had been in the middle of it. One man said to the other, "I don't know what we're going to do about Baptists and Johnson grass." His friend replied, "I don't know what we can do about the Baptists but I know what we can do about the Johnson grass. We can pour whiskey on it and Baptists will eat it down to a nub."

2. We Need the Rain

It's been so dry in West Texas that
The Baptists have started sprinkling,
The Methodists are using a wet wash cloth,
The Presbyterians are giving rain checks and,
The Catholics are turning wine back into water.
Now friends, that's DRY.

3. Pray for My Hearing

Boudreaux goes to the revival and listens to the preacher. After a while, the preacher asks anyone with needs to come forward and be prayed over. Boudreaux gets in line and when it's his turn the preacher says,

"Boudreaux, what do you want me to pray about?" Boudreaux says, "Preacher, I need you to pray for my hearing." So the preacher puts one finger in Boudreaux's ear and the other hand on top of his head and prays a while. After a few minutes, he removes his hands and says, "Boudreaux, how's your hearing now?" Boudreaux says, "I don't know preacher, it's not until next Wednesday in Opelousas."

4. Answered Prayer

A lady goes to her priest one day and tells him, "Father, I have a problem.

I have two female parrots, but they only know how to say one thing."

"What do they say?" the priest inquired.

"They say, 'Hi, we're hookers! Do you want to have some fun?'"

"That's obscene!" the priest exclaimed. Then he thought for a moment. "You know," he said. "I may have a solution to your problem. I have two male talking parrots, which I have taught to pray and read the Bible. Bring your two parrots over to my house, and we'll put them in the cage with Francis and Peter. My parrots can teach your parrots to praise and worship."

"Thank you," the woman responded. "This may very well be the solution."

The next day, she brought her female parrots to the priest's house. As he ushered her in, she saw that his two male parrots were inside their cage holding rosary beads and praying. Impressed, she walked over and placed her parrots in with them. After a few minutes, the female parrots cried out in unison, "Hi, we're hookers! Do you want to have some fun?" There was stunned silence.

Surprised, one male parrot looked over at the other male parrot and exclaimed, "Put the beads away, Frank. Our prayers have been answered."

5. An Important Person Here

Billy Graham was speaking in Florida, and they picked him up in a beautiful stretch limousine. It was the finest car he had ever seen. Following his speech, they were taking him back to the airport, and he said to the chauffeur, "Sir, this is the finest car I've ever seen in my life. Would you mind if I drive it?" The man said, "Mr. Graham, this is a very expensive car, and I am responsible for it. I'm not sure." Graham said, "I'll be very careful if you will just let me try."

So, the chauffeur got out, moved into the backseat, and let Graham beind the steering wheel. He got on the freeway, and his foot got a little heavy and was going 80 miles per hour when the patrolman pulled him over. He asked to see his driver's license, and he immediately recognized that it was Dr. Billy Graham. He went back to his car, radioed the dispatch office, and said to his superior, "Sir, I've got a very important person in a limousine pulled over, and I don't know what to do." The dispatcher asked, "Oh, is it Shaq?" The man replied, "No." The dispatcher said, "Well is it Governor Jeb Bush?" The man replied, "No." The dispatcher said, "Is it President Bush?" The man replied, "No." He said, "Well, who is it?" The man replied, "I don't know, sir. It may be Jesus, because

Billy Graham is his chauffeur."

6. Jesus and Deacons

A little boy became a Christian and an avid witness for Christ. He told everybody he met about Jesus and tried to win them to him. One day he walked up to an elderly man and said to him, "Sir, are you a Christian? Jesus can save you!"

The man said, "Son, I'll have you know, I'm the chairman of the deacons at my church." The little boy, not to be deterred, said, "That's OK. My Lord can fix anything."

7. Denominations

A woman goes to the post office to buy stamps for her Christmas cards.

She says to the clerk, "May I have 50 Christmas stamps?"

The clerk says, "What denomination?"

"Oh my gosh," the woman says, "Has it come to that? Give me 6 Catholic, 12 Lutheran, and 32 Baptist."

8. Church Gossip

The church gossip and self-appointed arbiter of the church's morals kept sticking her nose into other people's business. Several church members were unappreciative of her activities, but feared her enough to maintain their silence. She made a mistake, however, when she accused George, a new member, of being drunk after she saw his pickup truck parked in front of the town's only bar one afternoon. She commented to

George and others that everyone seeing it there would know what he was doing. George, a man of few words, stared at her for a moment and just walked away. He didn't explain, defend, or deny; he said nothing. Later that evening, George quietly parked his pickup in front of her house . . . and left it there all night.

9. Answered Prayer

Paddy was driving down the street in a sweat because he had an important meeting and couldn't find a parking place. Looking up to heaven, he said, "Lord take pity on me. If you find me a parking place I will go to Mass every Sunday for the rest of me life and give up me Irish Whiskey!" Miraculously, a parking place appeared. Paddy looked up again and said, "Never mind, I found one."

10. Baptists and Drinking

A cowboy, who is visiting Wyoming from Texas, walks into a bar and orders three mugs of Bud. He sits in the back of the room, drinking a sip out of each one in turn. When he finishes them, he comes back to the bar and orders three more. The bartender approaches and tells the cowboy, "You know, a mug goes flat after I draw it. It would taste better if you bought one at a time."

The cowboy replies, "Well, you see, I have two brothers. One is in Arizona, the other is in Colorado. When we all left our home in Texas, we promised that we'd drink this way to remember the days when we drank together. So I'm drinking one beer for each of my brothers and one for myself."

The bartender admits that this is a nice custom, and leaves it there. The cowboy becomes a regular in the bar and always drinks the same way. He orders three mugs and drinks them in turn. One day, he comes in and only orders two mugs. All the regulars take notice and fall silent. When he comes back to the bar for the second round, the bartender says, "I don't want to intrude on your grief, but I wanted to offer my condolences on your loss."

The cowboy looks quite puzzled for a moment, then a light dawns in his eyes and he says, "Oh, no, everyone's just fine," he explains. "It's just that my wife and I joined the Baptist church and I had to quit drinking. Hasn't affected my brothers though."

11. I'd Rather Lose a Methodist

A 90-year-old life-long Baptist was in the hospital, conscious, but without long to live. His family, who visited with him regularly, was surprised – no, shocked – to learn one day that he had called for the local Methodist minister and had joined the Methodist church. The family crowded around the hospital room demanding an explanation. "You've been a loyal Baptist all of your life. Why would you join the Methodist church here at the end of your life?"

"Well," he responded, "I figured since I was going to die soon, I would rather lose one of them than one of us!"

12. Circumcise a Bear

Three preachers were talking one day, and they said, "You know, we've preached to people all of our lives. I wonder what it would be like to preach to animals. They're God's creatures. He made them, and they can make some response." So one of them said to the other one, "Why don't we give it a try?" So they decided to go out in the woods, find a bear and preach to him and see what the response would be.

The Catholic priest went first. He came back a day or two later with cuts and scratches all over his body. They said, "How did you do?" He said, "Well, I started preaching to that bear, and he got mad, and he jumped on me and almost killed me. Luckily, I jerked out my Holy Water, sprinkled it on him and he calmed down, and everything seemed to be OK."

The Baptist preacher went next. He came back a few days later, and they asked how it went. He said, "Well, I found this bear and started preaching to it, and he got mad, and we started wrestling with one another, rolled down a hill into a stream of water, and I baptized that bear. He calmed down, and everything seemed to be OK."

The Jewish rabbi went next. He came back a few days later, cut and bruised and scratched all over, and they said, "How did it go?" He said, "Have you ever tried to circumcise a bear?"

13. There Is a Difference

A little Baptist boy and a little Catholic girl were playing one day (about 12 years old) and they decided to go skinny-dipping. So they took off their clothes and started into the water, and the little Baptist boy looked at her and said,

"You know, I never realized how much difference

there was between Catholics and Protestants."

14. Not Ready Now

A priest walks into a bar and asks the first man he meets, "Do you want to go to heaven?" The man says he does. "Then stand over there my son." The priest asks a second man, "Do you want to go to heaven?" The man says he does, so he joins the first guy. The priest walks up to another man and asks, "Do you want to go to heaven?"

"No, Father."

"You mean when you die, you don't want to go to heaven?"

"Oh, when I die," says the man. "I thought you were getting a group together to go right now."

15. No Nuns There

Three redneck construction workers went to a baseball game one day and bought themselves a couple of beers and leaned back to enjoy the ball game. Presently along came five nuns in their habits, including those big, wide white hats that they wear, and sat down in front of them. The men, of course, could hardly see over or around the habits and were disgruntled.

One said to the other, "Maybe we ought to go down to St. Michael's. I hear they have only three nuns there." Another replied, "Perhaps we ought to go to St. Mary's. I hear they only have two nuns down there." One of the sisters turned around, looked at them and said, "Why don't you go to hell? There are no nuns down there."

16. Four Religious Truths to Remember

Muslims do not recognize Jews as God's chosen people.

Jews do not recognize Jesus as the Messiah.

Protestants do not recognize the Pope as the leader of the Christian world.

Baptists do not recognize each other at the liquor store.

17. Long Sermons

It was an African American service and people were saying "Amen! Hallelujah! Amen!" One brother, after a period of time kept saying, "Amen, brother Pharaoh! Amen, Pharaoh!" After the service was over, the preacher cornered him and said, "What did you mean by saying, Pharaoh." He said, "God said to Pharaoh, 'Let my people go.'"

18. It's Time to Join

Doug was leaving church after Christmas services when Father McCarthy took him aside. "Douglas, my son," he said. "It's time you joined the Army of the Lord. We need to see you every Sunday."

"Then why do we only see you on Christmas and Easter?"

Doug looked to the right and to the left, and then leaned over to whisper in Father McCarthy's ear, "I'm in the Secret Service."

19. Don't Forget the Curlers

A nun walked up to the counter of a convenience store with a six pack in her hands. The clerk looked at her with a strange expression and the nun said, "It is for my hair." The clerk reached under the counter, pulled out a package of pretzels and said, "I understand sister. Don't forget the curlers."

20. How to Celebrate Christmas

Three little boys were talking one day about how they celebrated Christmas. One was a Baptist, the other a Catholic, and the third was a Jew.

The little Baptist boy said, "We gather around the Christmas tree on Christmas Eve, singing 'Silent Night, Holy Night' and then exchange gifts."

The little Catholic boy said, "We do about the same thing. We gather around the Christmas tree on Christmas Eve, sing 'Ava Marie' and then exchange gifts."

The little Jewish boy said, "Well we do about the same thing. We gather around the Christmas tree on Christmas Eve, count all the money we made at the store off of you Christians, and sing, 'What a Friend We Have in Jesus.'"

21. Religious Symbols

A teacher asked her grade-school students to bring a religious symbol the next day to school. A little Jewish boy brought the Star of David. A little Catholic boy brought a crucifix. A little Baptist boy brought a casserole.

22. God's Missing

In a certain suburban neighborhood, there were two brothers ages 8 and 10, and both were exceedingly mischievous. Whatever went wrong in the neighborhood, it turned out they had a hand in it. Their parents were at their wits' end trying to control them.

Hearing about a nearby priest who worked with delinquent boys, the mother suggested to the father that they ask the priest to talk with the boys. The father okayed it, and the mother went to the priest and made her request. He agreed, but said he wanted to see the youngest boy first and alone.

So the mother sent the youngest boy to the priest. The priest had the boy sit across from him as he sat behind his huge, impressive desk. For about 5 minutes they just sat and stared at each other. Finally, the priest pointed his forefinger at the boy and asked, "Where is God?"

The boy looked under the desk, in the corners of the room, all around, but found nothing. Again, louder, the priest pointed and asked, "Where is God?" Again the boy looked all around but found nothing. The priest leaned far across the desk and put his finger almost to the boy's nose and asked a third time, "WHERE IS GOD?" The boy panicked and ran all the way home.

Finding his older brother, he dragged him upstairs to their room. Trembling he said, "We are in BIIIIIIG trouble!"

The older brother asked, "What do you mean we are in BIIIIIIG trouble?"

His brother replied, "God is missing and they think WE did it!"

23. Being On Time

A physician in our community is a Roman Catholic

and has six children.

On Easter morning he and his family were driving to church when one of the small children leaned across the seat and said, "Dad, hurry." The father said, "Son, what's your hurry?" The boy replied, "This is Easter. It's the day Jesus will rise from the dead." His mother said, "That happened 2000 years ago." The boy replied, "O man! We're late for everything."

24. Do You Really Believe?

A televangelist went snow skiing. He was rather full of himself so he refused to take lessons. He simply strapped on the skis, mounted the ski lift, and headed for the top of the mountain. He passed the green station marking the spot where less experienced skiers disembarked. Then he passed the blue and didn't get off until he reached the turnaround at the black station.

Off the chair he came. Down the hill he flew, end over end to the first turn, which he didn't take. He sailed over a cliff into a yawning gorge. About ten feet down, he miraculously grabbed a tree branch. There he hung, suspended over certain death. He yelled at the top of his lungs, "Is anybody up there?" It so happened that a renowned "liberal" minister, who caught constant flak from the televangelist for his "godless" beliefs, had witnessed the entire scene.

The liberal stayed out of the televangelist's view and called down to him, "Yes, there is someone up here. It is I, the Lord your God. The time of your testing is at hand. If you truly believe as you so often proclaim, simply let go and I shall send my angels to catch thee."

There was a deadly silence from below. Then came the haunting question, "Is anybody else up there?"

27. Texan Joining a Church

An old Texan went to an East Texas church and asked to join. The preacher said, "Ok, but you have to pass a small Bible test first. The first question is where was Jesus born?"

The man answered, "Longview."

The preacher said, "Sorry, you can't join our church."

So he went to another church and asked to join. The preacher said, "We would love to have you, but you have to pass a Bible test first. Where was Jesus born?"

The man said, "Tyler."

The preacher said, "Sorry, you can't join our church."

So he goes to another church and asks to join. The preacher said, "That's great; we welcome you with open arms."

The man said, "I don't have to pass no Bible test first?"

The preacher said, "No."

The man said, "Can I ask a question? Where was Jesus born?"

The preacher said, "Palestine."

The man mumbled to himself, "I knew it was in East Texas somewhere."

28. Catholic Gasoline

Sister Mary Ann, who worked for a home health agency, was out making her rounds visiting home-bound patients when she ran out of gas. As luck would have it, an Exxon Gasoline station was just a block away. She walked to the station to borrow a gas can and bought some gas. The attendant told her that the only gas can he owned had been loaned out. Since Sister Mary Ann was on the way to see a patient, she decided not to wait and walked back to her car. She looked for something in her car that she could fill with gas and spotted the bedpan she was taking to the patient. Always resourceful, Sister Mary Ann carried the bedpan to the station, filled it with gasoline, and carried the full bedpan back to her car. As she was pouring the gas into her tank, two Baptists watched from across the street. One of them turned to the other and said, "If it starts, I'm turning Catholic."

Chapter 9

Politics

1. Politicians — Do You Know Me?

Lawyers should never ask a Southern grandma a question if they aren't prepared for the answer! In a trial, a Southern small-town prosecuting attorney called his first witness, a grandmotherly, elderly woman to the stand. He approached her and asked, "Mrs. Jones, do you know me?"

She responded, "Why, yes, I do know you, Billy Joe. I've known you since you were a young boy, and frankly, you've been a big disappointment to me. You lie, you cheat on your wife, and you manipulate people and talk about them behind their backs. You think you're a big shot when you haven't the brains to realize you never will amount to anything more than a two-bit paper pusher. Yes, I know you."

The lawyer was stunned! Not knowing what else to do, he pointed across the room and asked, "Mrs. Jones, do you know the defense attorney?"

She again replied, "Why, yes, I do. I've known Eugene since he was a youngster, too. He's lazy, bigoted, and he has a drinking problem. He can't build a normal relationship with anyone and his law practice is one of the worst in the entire state. Not to mention he cheated on his wife with three different women. One of them was your wife. Yes, I know him."

The defense attorney almost died.

The judge asked the counselors to approach the bench and, in a very quiet voice, said, "If either of you idiots asks her if she knows me, I'll have you cited for contempt of court."

2. Don't Be Late

A priest was being honored at his retirement dinner after 25 years serving the parish.

A leading local politician and member of the congregation was chosen to make the presentation and give a little speech at the dinner. He was late getting there, so the priest decided to say his own few words while they waited.

"I got my first impression of the parish from the very first confession I heard here. I thought I had been assigned to a terrible place. The very first person that entered my confessional told me that he had stolen a television set and, when questioned by the police, was able to lie his way out of it. He has stolen money from his parents, embezzled from his employer, had an affair with his boss's wife, and took illegal drugs. I was appalled. But as the days went on I knew that my people were not all like that and I had, indeed, come to a fine parish full of good and loving people."

Just as the priest finished his talk, the politican arrived full of apologies at being late. He immediately began to make the presentation and gave his talk.

"I'll never forget the first day our parish priest arrived," said the politician. "In fact, I had the honor of being the very first person to go to him for confession."

3. Easy to Operate On

Five surgeons are discussing who makes the best patient to operate on. The first surgeon says, "I like to see accountants on my operation table, because when you open them up, everything inside is numbered."

The second responds, "Yeah, but you should try electricians! Everything inside them is color-coded."

The third surgeon says, "No, I really think file clerks are the best, everything inside them is in alphabetical order."

The fourth surgeon chimes in: "You know, I like construction workers. Those guys always understand when you have a few parts left over at the end, and when the job takes longer than you said it would."

But the fifth surgeon shut them all up when he observed: "You're all wrong. Politicians are the easiest to operate on. There's no guts, no heart, and no spine, and the head and tail are interchangeable."

4. He's Going to Be a Congressman

An old country preacher had a teenage son, and it was getting time the boy should give some thoughts to choosing a profession. Like many young men, the boy didn't really know what he wanted to do, and he didn't seem too concerned about it. One day, while the boy was away at school, his father decided to try an experiment. He went into the boy's room and placed on his study table three objects: a Bible, a silver dollar and a bottle of whiskey. I'll just hide behind the door," the old preacher said to himself, "and when he comes home from school this afternoon, I'll see which object he picks up. If it's the Bible, he's going to be a preacher like me, and what a blessing that would be! If he picks up the dollar, he's going to be a gambler. If he picks up the whiskey, he's going to be a no-good drunkard, and Lord, what a shame that would be." The old man waited anxiously, and soon heard his son's footsteps as he entered the house whistling and headed for his room. He tossed his books on the bed, and as he turned to leave the room he spotted the objects on the table. With curiosity in his eye, he walked over to inspect them. Finally, he picked up the Bible and placed it under his arm. He picked up the silver dollar and dropped it into his pocket. He uncorked the bottle and took a big drink. "Lord have mercy," the old man whispered, "He's gonna be a congressman!"

5. The Smartest Guy in the World

There were four men on a plane when the motors ran out, and it was obvious that the plane was going to crash. The pilot came out of the cockpit, and said, "Men, this plane is going down, and I am going to jump. There are four of you and only three parachutes. You'll have to decide among yourselves who is going to be left with the plane."

One was a doctor, one was a preacher, one was a congressman, and the other was a college student. The doctor grabbed a parachute and said, "Men, I am a doctor and I have spent my life helping people. I can't afford to go down with this plane. I am taking a parachute and jumping out the door." And out the door he went.

The congressman grabbed the next pack, threw it on his back, and said, "I'm the smartest man in the world. The world can't get along without me. I am taking this and jumping." And out the door he went.

The preacher then turned to the young man, and said, "Son, I am a man of God, and I am ready to go. I've lived a rich, full life. You take the last parachute, and I'll stay with the plane." The young man responded, "No need to worry. The smartest man in the world just jumped with my backpack on his back."

6. Prayer and Taxes

A little boy wanted $100 very badly and prayed for weeks but nothing happened. Then he decided to write a letter to the Lord requesting the $100. When the postal authorities received the letter addressed to the Lord, USA, they decided to send it to The President.

The President was so impressed, touched, and amused that he instructed his secretary to send the little boy a $5 bill. The President thought this would appear to be a lot of money to a little boy.

The little boy was delighted with the $5 and sat down to write a thank-you note to the Lord, which read.

Dear Lord,

Thank you very much for sending me the money. However, I noticed that for some reason you had to send it through Washington, DC, and as usual, those thieving politicians deducted $95.

7. Not in Your District

Years ago, Senator Everett Dirkson from Illinois, was running for the senate. A young college student came up to him and said, "Mr. Dirkson, I wouldn't vote for you if you were St. Peter." The Senator in his usual witty way said, "Son, if I were St. Peter you couldn't vote for me. You would not be in my district."

8. Living with the Laws

The reason congressmen try so hard to get re-elected is that they would hate to have to make a living under the laws they've passed.